Austin Mardon   Brey Dawson

Robert Mcweeny   Zach Schauer

Riley Witiw

DARK NIGHT COMETH

Antarctic
Institute
AIC of Canada

Typeset, cover and illustration by Josh Harnack

ISBN 978-1-77369-146-6
Golden Meteorite Press
103 11919 82 St NW
Edmonton, AB T5B 2W3
www.goldenmeteoritepress.com

Antarctic
Institute
AIC of Canada

The Brain—is wider than the Sky—
For—put them side by side—
The one the other will contain
With ease—and you—beside—
The Brain is deeper than the sea—
For—hold them—Blue to Blue—
The one the other will absorb—
As sponges—Buckets—do—
The Brain is just the weight of God—
For—Heft them—Pound for Pound—
And they will differ—if they do—
As Syllable from Sound—

Emily Dickinson, c. 1862

Table of Contents

Prologue 1

   1922 .... *3*

Brainsick 5

   Psychotic Breaks *9*

Onset and Onwards 11

Rising Tension 16

   Antarctica *16*

   Moscow *21*

The Break 26

   The Bar *29*

False Admission to the Hospital 32

Wandering in the Descent of My Insanity 36

To the ER and Beyond 42

My Father's First Visit 47

Boredom – Months Of 51

Trails by, Trails of Fire 56

The Rebirth of My Old Life 62

What Now? 67

Epilogue: what Now? Again. 71

DARK NIGHT COMETH

Prologue

"Once in the dark of night / Inflamed with love and yearning, I arose / (O coming of delight!) / And went, as no one knows / When all my house lay long in deep repose."
St. John of the Cross, The Dark Night of the Soul

This book is an analysis of Dr. Austin Mardon's experience with psychosis and schizophrenia, as well as the story about the death and resurrection of a brilliant young academic's life. In relaying Austin's experience, it is not always clear what is "real" and what is a symptom of mental illness; therefore, this text does not necessarily seek to depict objective reality, but rather, reality as Austin experienced it.

At the end of our first interview with Austin, I asked him if there was anything he wanted to say about the book or his experience with psychosis in general. Austin, always the talker, began answering before I could even finish the question. Ordinarily, his off-the-cuff interruptions are the direct result of overflowing knowledge, relevant experience, and enthusiasm – it's quite endearing. But this time, he sounded much more deliberate than usual:

"Whenever I'm doing a speech about my life, large segments can be a real downer with lots of negativity," he ponders. "But ultimately, it's a story of hope and redemption. I have probably had a much better and socially-productive life as a schizophrenic than I ever would have if I wasn't touched by mental illness."

He's not wrong. But if you saw Austin on the street, he probably wouldn't fit your archetypal visualization of a successful person. At 6'5 and somewhere around 350 pounds, he has difficulty finding clothes that fit, but as a self-described 'hippie,' he doesn't really care.

You'll typically see him in a loose-fitting collared shirt and simple black shorts held-up by suspenders, donning the same pair of tired Nikes that, I suspect, he was born in. However, he does credit his wife Catherine for reigning in his scraggly hair and large, snowy beard into something a tad more refined. Still, Austin's appearance doesn't allude to his long list of awards and honours, including but not limited to the Order of Canada medal, membership in the Royal Society of Canada, and the Antarctic Service Medal from the US Congress. It does not suggest Austin's membership in the Explorer's Club of New York (the premier society for world explorers) or the International Academy of Astronautics, headquartered in Paris, France.

His condo is modest and is located in the heart of one of Edmonton's most troubled districts. Both he and Catherine are disabled, rendering the space to be a few notches less clean than they'd probably prefer. The clutter, however, is quite interesting to peruse through and reflects the creative and prolific lives of its owners. The wall is dotted with Catherine's unusual musical instruments (a bodhran, strum, travelling mandolin – to name a few), photographs of Austin posing with all sorts of Popes and politicians, coffee shop posters, and a small display containing several of Austin's medals.

A bookcase in the back overflows with over 200 books that Austin and Catherine have authored. The hall to their kitchen is populated with countless degree certificates staggered somewhat haphazardly through the wall: undergrads, masters, doctorates, honorary degrees – both Austin and Catherine have the kind of qualifications that would usually be framed in illustrious mansions rather than humble apartments.

Yet, in lieu of some sort of affluent lifestyle, Austin knows that he really has it all (and ironically, more so than many of his able-bodied peers) – his loving marriage, a recently paid-off home, a staggeringly expansive network of people who care about him, and even an ill-behaved but well-meaning family dog (and son, Austin jokes). He has had a remarkable impact in a variety of academic fields and in mental health advocacy. Senior and high-profile politicians frequently request Austin's input, even when he plays the dissident.

When Austin lost his cognition in the early 90s, he believed he would never experience these milestones. After all, who was he to doubt the physicians, colleagues, and family members who assured him his life was over?

In 1992, Austin's life came to an end.

1992

When Austin opened the door of the bar bathroom to return to his seat, everything changed:

The girls by the bar dressed in black?

"Oh, they're witches! Witches!" realized Austin.

It seemed like the witches were trying to signal something to him. He figured there must be a symbolic connection between the colour black and the witches' coven. He started recognizing that other bar patrons were in on it, as well.

There was no time to worry about the coven – Austin was swatting at the bees buzzing all around him.

But then the bar's TV started blaring at Austin, projecting images of the moon directly into his mind. The bees didn't seem so important anymore.

"Wow, I'm in the moon. The moon is me," thought Austin, encapsulated by the documentary's graphical beauty.

Austin's identification with the documentary began accelerating. It started to take hold in Austin's mind that he could control the video and the direction of the program's narration with his thoughts.

At this point, Austin recalls a fading voice saying, "hello, something is wrong" before giving in to his perception of the reality around him.
This was the beginning of his 'dark night of the soul' – only, one that would last the next 15 years.

Brainsick

"It was almost as if nothing worse could happen to me. The doctor thought I'd be homeless for the next 25 years."

Austin sat up from the cranny of his sunken leather couch, fidgeting pensively. "Sometimes I hear things that are real that I think are hallucinations," he says. "And sometimes I hear hallucinations that I think are real. What happens is you can't trust your senses."

Austin then got a familiar look in his eye – it screamed he was about to enjoy a bout of intelligent misbehaviour. Looking bashfully at his son, Stanley, Austin toyed, "Stan, are you really there? Am I talking to a real person on Zoom?"

Stanley, one of Austin's adopted adult sons, unleashed a cartoonish cackle before gawking back with his trademark retort, "shut up."

I smiled through my webcam at the two of them. Having witnessed another classic 'Austin moment,' I felt warmth. I am happy talking with these people about their lives – I am grateful for my boss.

It can be easy to forget that Austin has psychosis. Complementary to his awards and accolades are a vibrant personality and intellect. Austin is intimidatingly smart, memorizing swaths of religious scripture and scientific text – citing templars and taxonomy in everyday conversation. However, the titles that affirm his giftedness (PhD, CM, LLD) are absent from his medical file. There, they are placeholders for a different yet unequivocally powerful abbreviation: 'SCV' – schizophrenia.

Psychosis is a term used to describe mental illnesses that disrupt one's sense of reality. This disruption often presents with delusional thinking, hallucinations, and disorganized speech. Schizophrenia – Austin's diagnosis – is a psychotic illness characterized by delusions, hallucinations, and changes in behaviour that last for longer than six months. For Austin, when the doctors defined him, they redefined almost every aspect of his daily life.

Schizophrenia has been colloquialized in western culture. As a result, many people tend to identify any psychotic behaviour as 'schizophrenic.' Our society is reasonably good at identifying psychotic symptoms in the outwardly ill, but individuals in-crisis may be mislabeled 'schizo' by the unenlightened. This is presumptuous and often incorrect – after all, we do not use the term 'breast-cancer' to refer to other cancers. We should depart from labelling that employs a 'same-shit-different-pile' approach.

The truth is, a break from reality may originate from one of several psychotic disorders. Psychosis is an umbrella term under which schizophrenia is one of many titles. As a society, we should use medical terminology correctly, and more importantly, avoid appropriating it.

For instance, psychotic symptoms may arise from mania – drastic mood elevations in Bipolar patients. With mood disturbance, psychosis may indicate Schizoaffective Disorder, which includes schizophrenia symptoms but is distinct. Psychotic delusions and hallucinations can occur after using recreational drugs – a condition called Drug-Induced Psychosis. Additionally, seemingly unrelated health conditions such as thyroid disease, auto-immune disorders, and Huntington's disease could potentially cause Psychotic Disorder due to another medical condition.

"The capabilities of your mind change after you develop schizophrenia" sighs Austin. "The operating parameters – they're just different."

Austin is right. The brain undergoes drastic changes in neurochemistry during and following a psychotic event – but for different reasons.

During an episode of psychosis, the brain is overloaded by stress, initiating cascades of altered neural circuit function. This stress may arise in many ways – perhaps caused by a family member's death, or through experiencing physical or emotional trauma. For many patients, including Austin, psychosis is not begotten by a single triggering event. In fact, only a handful of patients develop psychosis due to stressful experiences.

The fact that psychosis is not caused by one traumatic event raises an important question: Why might some people be predisposed to psychosis while others are not? The answer is not decisive. Researchers speculate that genetics, environmental factors, and lived experience combine to create brain-states that make psychosis possible. The exact formula is not well understood, but it is generally accepted that satisfying certain criteria in these areas may put someone at higher risk for developing a psychotic disorder.

For Austin, schizophrenia created stressors that drained his intellectual faculties, but he also experienced a nosedive in cognition after beginning treatment with antipsychotic medications. Austin feels more lucid, but cognitively neutered since being treated with antipsychotics and neuroleptics. This is a common grievance among psychosis sufferers. While the meds are often essential for treatment, they are not without adverse and inconvenient side effects – more on that later in this book.

I lean back in my chair and briefly shut my eyes, haphazardly attempting to construct a probably over-zealous incantation of the question 'what is psychosis?' And so I ask, "what is psychosis? One could answer the question in many ways: It's a medical condition, it's an experience – it's many things. What is psychosis to Austin Mardon?"

I'm unsure how Austin will answer, but, having known him for a while, I've come to expect some predictable eccentricities in his answers.

First, I expect Austin to covertly expand my mind through some off-kilter explanation that happens to be shockingly bang-on in its relevance and insight.

"It was like a point or rite of passage from one part of my life to a different part. Everything that I learned, everything that I was going towards, everything from the first part of my life ended at that point – the collapse," proverbializes Austin. "After that, I had to pick up the pieces and go into a world that many people don't go into or do very well in. It was like a very clear demarcation point in my life – before and after. Ironically, I probably did better as a person with schizophrenia than before as a researcher.

I think it's because I use the same skills as a scientist and as a scholar to function."

Second, he will segue from his precedent-shattering introduction to something slightly less relevant – likely a story from his past. I will be thoroughly confused by this shift, assuming fault for lacking the comprehension needed to trace the anecdote's relevance.

"After, it was as if nothing worse could happen to me. I was told my life was over. The doctor thought I'd be homeless for the next 25 years. I had a very bad prognosis, but it hasn't been like that," says Austin. "It hasn't been necessarily easy, and I haven't had a normative life, which jars on a lot of people because they don't understand. They either want me institutionalized or somehow locked away. They can't ever see why I've taken a different path that a lot of people don't take. I could be a millionaire and it still wouldn't improve my life as much as a new medication. I do have the luxury of living in a society that does support the disabled. I've always been very grateful. A lot of people aren't grateful, I find. They're very resentful and stuff, but I was never resentful. I don't like it when the rules conflict or don't make sense."

My confusion arrives on schedule.

Finally, I expect him to reaffirm the initial parable, state something that seems obvious, and summarize with an off-the-cuff idiom worthy of publication in a philosophy text.

"Psychosis is like a break from reality, and you can't trust any of your senses. You can well imagine if you can't trust any of your senses, how difficult that would be to function," he explains. "I tell other people with schizophrenia that you can't judge yourself by your parents or society because your operating parameters are different. A lot of people say, 'well, it's about money and stuff,' but to be honest, I think health is a lot more valuable than money. You just need to have enough money to live on. I never left the period of being a starving student, I became a starving psychotic."

jaws drop audibly, standing ovation, the crowd goes wild

Austin says it perfectly, dodging neurological esoterics in favour of something more humanistic. Psychosis is a rite of passage to a different life, a paradigm shift, a loss of innocence. My mental conception of Austin suddenly begins to reorganize, overtaken by metaphor. He is a griffin – reawakened from till and smoulder. A lamb born to toil, reborn to triumph. A man who rose.

Psychotic Breaks

The term 'Psychotic Break' is a common expression used to describe what medical professionals call a 'Psychotic Episode.' For our purposes, the terms are used interchangeably to best illustrate the contexts of Austin's decline.

Austin remembers pieces of his psychotic break – the point at which his reality faltered most consummately. However, accurately recalling a psychotic event is virtually impossible. This reality created challenges in extracting information from Austin – information that would allow us to write sections of this book that recount his madness.

Psychiatry has long understood psychosis to discolour human memory. A quick neuroscientific foray – psychotic episodes damage the frontal and temporal lobe regions, hindering one's ability to make associations. Damage to these substrates does not merely obstruct recollection of the psychotic experience. Instead, it endangers broader memory functions.

Austin isn't without his forgetful moments, sometimes telephoning his students, forgetting why he had called – an endearing fault, but understandably troublesome. Regardless, Austin gets along quite well, managing to keep an overfilled schedule while remembering nitty-gritty's about his friends and coworkers. His propensity to memorize details about others would put most psychotherapists to shame. Still, Austin has his hazy days.

A psychotic break certainly sounds like an event – something sudden; breakneck and visceral. Austin views it with more nuance. He explains, "from what I understand, it can either happen slowly, gradually, or have a rapid break like I did. Just snap – like a seizure almost. So the duration of the total disintegration can be over months or years, or it can be instantaneous as mine was."

Austin is correct. Memoirs, case-studies, and medical texts confirm psychotic episodes to be either headlong, plodding, or somewhere in-between. Austin's may have been just that, but his recall suggests a sudden jamming of his cognition.

Prior, Austin experienced prodromal symptoms – early signs of the inevitable downcast. Because of this, Austin's journey toward neurocognitive malice was long and winding. Ergo, the malice was predetermined.

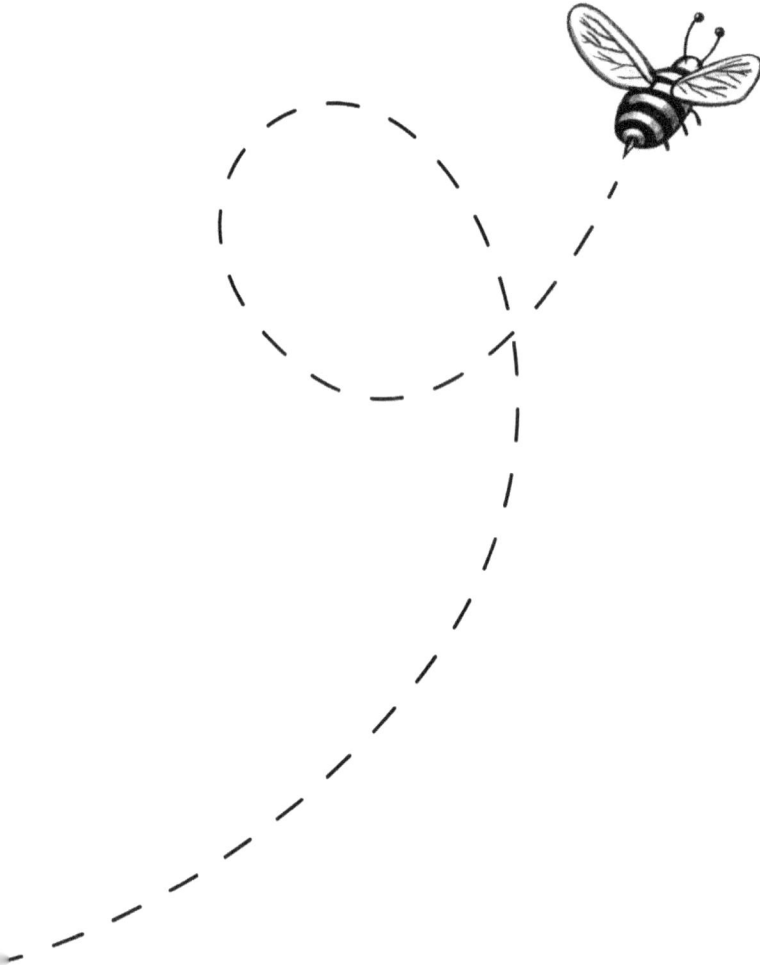

Onset and Onwards

"Unseen in the background, Fate was quietly slipping lead into the boxing-glove."
P.G. Wodehouse, A Wodehouse Bestiary

Austin's thoughts rapidly shift through different topics as the interview progresses. We bounce back and forth, discussing how girls are "his kryptonite," gush about our favourite coffee spots, and the movie The Beautiful Mind. That is all well and good, but every time I try to guide our conversation back to Austin's early schizophrenia symptoms (the topic he chose for this interview), he pauses and gives a short 'yes' or 'no' answer.

At age 58, after thousands of medication injections, a cognitive haze now blankets Austin's complicated upbringing – complications, which probably cloaked early warning signs of what was to come. Given that Austin's mother, May, has schizophrenia, it may not be totally shocking that Austin followed suit, and one might expect that Austin's parents would have been even more attentive to the symptoms of schizophrenia in their children. But, of course, it is never that simple.

Perhaps it was denial. Austin's father, Ernest, was very defensive of May and any comments about her worsening mental condition and schizophrenia diagnosis. Austin remembers that his father would usually downplay her psychotic outbursts, refusing to let her withstand any criticism – even during her manic bouts of verbal abuse that would leave the family reeling and divided. Sometimes his father would even defend the abuse, telling Austin it was "his duty as the first born child to take the abuse and not complain."

For whatever reason, Ernest found it simpler to reprimand his children for "provoking" May, rather than acknowledging that they did nothing to beget her cutting tongue, which was undoubtedly a symptom of her schizophrenia.

Similarly, it is possible Ernest chose not to read into Austin's plainly evident prodromal symptoms as a child – the first of three phases of symptoms that occur throughout an individual's journey with schizophrenia. Broadly speaking, they are unusual behaviours that become present when an individual is at risk for psychosis.

In our current age, recognizing these subtle changes in a person's behaviour and interceding with the proper antipsychotic medication can help alleviate symptoms more successfully in the long-term. Our capability for this is a wondrous progression in the field of psychiatry. Unfortunately for Austin, even if he had been diagnosed as a child, the available medications and treatments during those days would not have elicited anywhere near the same results. It was not until the mid 90s that antipsychotic medication leaped forward.

It is difficult for Austin to time-stamp his anecdotes with regard to which psychotic phase they occurred in, but after pouring through hours of interviews, it is clear he went through it all the same. One early sign seen in Austin's childhood was his active withdrawal from many social interactions due to his "odd" personality. He recalls, "there were features of my childhood that were very common to pre-schizophrenia in hindsight – you could say that my social isolation and social disconnection were tied with schizophrenia."

Other prodromal behaviours were becoming evident later on during Austin's adulthood. In particular, he developed intense anxiety over the academic career and relationships he had started to build, culminating in a crushing fear of failure. Austin hoped that earning a PhD would allow him to follow in the footsteps of his father and grandfather. He reflects, "I tried so hard for that, I drove myself crazy."

He was also strung up on the fact that his girlfriend did not want to be with him anymore. "I felt overwhelmed. I felt a sense of failure because my girlfriend had broken up with me," says Austin, beginning to chuckle. "That's the thing that gets me – girls."

The second phase is defined by active schizophrenic symptoms.

These symptoms are the most visible and are usually telltale warnings of psychosis. Individuals tend to be suffering the worst from hallucinations and delusions during this time frame, therefore being the stage where people become officially diagnosed with schizophrenia. During this period, Austin was in the throes of an affective disorder that made his emotions and expressions persistently flat – a common symptom during the active phase.

The delusions and hallucinations became pervasive. While enjoying coffee and a cinnamon bun at his local coffee shop, Austin started having strange interactions with the television. "They had a game playing on the TV, and I thought, 'woah, I can control the game,'" Austin explains. "And I was just staring at the game, without blinking, controlling where the puck goes. But then the team lost."

Other hallucinations were less mild and decidedly more troubling: "I thought there werewolves on the moon, and I felt like howling at the moon," says Austin.

The third phase embodies residual schizophrenia symptoms. During this phase, individuals continue to have symptoms even after their psychosis has subsided. These symptoms tend to be more muted, similar to the prodromal symptoms, such as the inability to think logically. Austin suffered from this stage in particular. He reminisces, "I lost 50 IQ points, so I couldn't think properly. I couldn't talk logically and think logically."

Another symptom is eccentric behaviour, and let me tell you, Austin is the most eccentric guy you'll ever meet. He once got banned from Library and Archives Canada (how is that even possible?) because, on multiple occasions, he brought them boxes of receipts to sort and organize. "It's a way of compensating for the hoarding," Austin laughs. "You are expanding by getting other people to hoard for you."

Let it be known that the spending habits and eccentric behaviour of Austin Mardon are now chronicled in Canadian history, much to the dismay and annoyance of junior bureaucrats.

So, after briefly covering the onset and development of Austin's schizophrenia, attentive readers will likely ask two questions. First, "now that I know the symptoms, what is it like to experience schizophrenia?" by which, they mean something like: we loosely understand the science, but what does it look and feel like to actually be schizophrenic? The second question arising is probably, "and what happened with Austin Mardon?"
The answer to both questions: the experience of schizophrenia and chronology of Dr. Mardon is the purpose of the book – to capture, in a word (Austin's word to be exact), the "poetic awesomeness" of his experience of schizophrenia. Now, we must remind the reader that we are not glorifying or romanticizing the very real challenges that people with schizophrenia face. We are showing that Austin's experience was literally poetic awesomeness. That is, Austin's story is one worth writing down because it inspires a feeling of awe and wonder about life's journey, the human desire not just to live but to strive, and the mysteries of human consciousness. One should marvel at the intricacies of Austin's unusual adventures and expansive mind without forgetting the real obstacles he and many other people with schizophrenia hurl over like they are pole vaulting Olympus.

Now that the setting has been outlined, the main character revealed, and the foreshadowing of the coming conflict announced, we are ready to unveil the action of the story – Austin's slow onset, his psychotic break, and his heroic recovery.

Rising Tension

"Reality is the leading cause of stress amongst those in touch with it."
Trudy, The Search for Signs of Intelligence in the Universe

Antarctica

While a spry, youthful child, Austin was an explorer with wonder in his heart. He decided to pursue a life of learning, in part to earn Ernest's approval, who was a medievalist at the University of Lethbridge. But more than that, Austin was inspired by all the figures he heard of from his father. From ancient historians like Herodotus, to philosophers of antiquity like St. Thomas Aquinas, to literary geniuses like Shakespeare and Joyce, all the way to the science fiction of Asimov, Heinlein, and Clarke, Austin fell in love with books and learning, even though the idea of academia scared him when he started taking it seriously.

Ernest shepherded Austin through this foreign terrain, shaping his intellectual footsteps. Eventually, after years under his father's tutelage, only vaguely understanding works from Chaucer and Christian mystics, Austin finally enrolled in the University of Lethbridge. Landing on Geography, Austin found a specialty as obscure as his father's – just as underrated, and perfect for his sense of adventure brought on by stories in scripture and unravelling in Tolkien.

After Austin finished his undergrad at the University of Lethbridge at age 24, he was invited to join an Antarctic expedition led by Dr. William A. Cassidy – a meteorite hunter and professor emeritus at the University of Pittsburgh. Austin had caught Dr. Cassidy's attention by publishing a book suggesting the use of remote sensing to detect meteorites.

In many ways, this invitation was quite literally a dream come true for a freshly graduated Austin, blooming in his life's prime. Even more, the invitation was essentially a career-maker that would allow Austin to become a sought-after voice in his field and an otherwise successful academic.

However, fate had something quite different in mind. Yes, the expedition would be life-changing, but primarily in ways that defied expectation.

To say Antarctica was an adventure is an understatement. In recounting the events, Austin shakes his head and looks down. "People still don't understand," says Austin. "It was like going to the moon or something. It was like seeing the face of God. Part of me never left Antarctica, I don't think."

Antarctica is famously brutal and unforgiving. In fact, Antarctica is so tough on explorers' mental health, that Jack Stuster wrote a book, Bold Endeavors, claiming that studying people who stay long term in Antarctica will provide evidence on the experience astronauts will face whilst travelling seven months along in equally unforgiving space toward Mars. A grande expanse of blinding snow covering barren landscapes of sheer ice littered with crevasses that extend 150 feet into the centre of the Earth, Antarctica is winter par excellence. Dante described the ninth, innermost circle of hell as a "prison of ice," and William Blake's famous illustration Gates of Hell depicts two figures standing in front of an entrance – inside the entranceway, we see jagged icicles spiking from the ground.

Like all memorable stories of adventure, our young hero journeyed from his small hovel in Lethbridge, Alberta, to a remote, dangerous, distant, and (literally) uncharted territory. Our explorer of the unknown recounted the words of a veteran helicopter pilot who briefed him and his fellow researchers, warning them that their time in the world's most southern continent would be more stressful than his three tours in Vietnam combined. And so it was.

The consistent and blistering cold defined a great deal of the experience. When the researchers woke up, they spent their mornings unfreezing the food from the previous day. After warming up pots of food for breakfast and lunch, it would not take long for the leftovers to freeze back up again. It was a monotonous, albeit necessary, process. Says Austin, "I was eating about 4000 calories a day, yet I lost about 50 pounds."

So, how does one motivate a group of young men in such tumultuous circumstances?

"We had as much liquor as wanted. It was great," laughs Austin.
He describes camping as a huge party but with a visceral sense of adventure. Austin recounts, "It was like Star Wars or something. When I told that to Bill Cassidy, he got pissed off. He said, 'this isn't an adventure, this is serious.'"

Austin says that, in turn, he apologized to Bill, but judging from his goofy smile even as he reminisces about the story 40 years later, one questions the sincerity of his supposedly regretful acknowledgement. Sure, these guys were out there having near-death experiences in a frozen wasteland, but they were also having fun. After all, the hero in a good adventure never fully comprehends the danger of their situation. Luke Skywalker wants to leave Tatooine because he is excited and dreams about flying through the far reaches of space. Simba, despite all warning from his father, wanders innocently through the forest and naively explores the kingdom that is his under the spell of pure curiosity, until he accidentally stumbles upon the Elephant Graveyard.

One particularly saccharine moment came quite unexpectedly for Austin. "I was taking a leak," he notes jovially.

Then, the Dutch scientist, Luke Lindler, started screaming at Austin and waving his arms. Austin, understandably perplexed in a moment of privacy, thought, "what the hell?"

It turns out Lindler had a point:

"You idiot, you're pissing on a meteorite! On a meteorite! What the hell are you doing?" screamed Lindler.

In our interview, Austin remarks that if in 50 years, they discover evidence of life in a meteorite on the moon, you – the reader – will know that it is, in fact, Austin's urine. Over the course of the expedition, the team found over 700 meteorites, including some that were carbonaceous and lunar.

But throughout the goofy moments and excitement was a dark reality: the physiological and psychological stresses were mounting up and taking a toll on Austin's mental health. His psyche was secretly creeping up to the badlands from which no one returns, and Austin was, at the time, unaware of the impact it would have on him.

The stresses became matters of life and death in the truest sense of the phrase. During the third day of the expedition, Austin nearly fell into a deep crevasse, accelerating on his snowmobile as the ground caved in beneath him – basically just levitating above a bottomless pit. His once familiar land of joyous exploration was literally crumbling beneath his feet.

Pursuing treasure in a faraway land, like the allure of new science found in the study of ancient meteorites in a frozen hearth, often requires sacrifice. Luke Skywalker loses his arm in his first brush with Darth Vader, and Austin, too, lost parts of his body – with the exception that no robot doctors could build him a new arm. The extreme cold never relented, subjecting Austin to lifelong injuries he still has today, including a frozen lung and nerve damage to his feet due to frostbite. The entire trip, Austin also suffered high altitude sickness, with blood coming out of his eyes, nose, and urine. When Austin asked Dr. Cassidy if such symptoms were serious, he replied, "stop complaining, Austin. You're a wimp. My toenails just fell off last night."

Yuck.

Indeed, bodily harm is a common side effect of adventuring in the Antarctic. In our conversation, Austin noted that, according to the Explorer's Club, most people who go down to Antarctica become disabled afterwards. Unfortunately for Austin, he was suffering more than just physical ailments. The trauma began to affect his mind. The event that really sticks out to Austin is when he was trying to count meteorites, but couldn't think past the number seven. It was the first crack in his cognition – perhaps one that would not have led to anything more if it had not been for the events that were soon to follow.

Austin's prodromal symptoms were the foreshadow of the oncoming journey to the underworld he would have to encounter. In Antarctica, Austin received the black spot, the symbol, originating in Treasure Island, that something was chasing after him. Or better yet, like Jack Sparrow, the Kraken was chasing him, ready to follow him to the ends of the earth to swallow him in the depths of Davy Jones' locker.

Nonetheless, Austin's journey was an overall success, our hero acquired the treasure. Austin left Antarctica with meteorites, accolades, such as entrance into the prestigious Explorer's Club in New York City, and a story he could never forget. "Antarctica crippled me mentally and physically, but it was my finest hour," says Austin, chest-swelled and beaming.

Little did he know, the Kraken had already snagged him. He was already on his way to the underworld. "Antarctica was like the edge of the world, and Moscow was the dark centre of the world," Austin foreshadows in our interview.

One day, in Moscow, Austin would wake up with the realization that he was in Davy Jones' locker, that he had been consumed by a Leviathan, and sunk to the bottom of the ocean. But Austin was not there... yet.

Moscow

In March 1991, Austin was 29 years old. Antarctica had become a memory of the past. He was sitting at home reading his daily mail when he received a letter from the Geographical Society of the USSR inviting him on an expedition to Novaya Zemlya – an archipelago in the Arctic.

Austin had already been shortlisted once, in 1988, on a trek to the North Pole by the Soviet government due to his lack of physical endurance. The Soviets had travelled to the Arctic on skis, and so denied the simple Canadian scientist with brains and less brawn the opportunity to join the expedition.

So, when Austin received notice that he could once again study with Soviets and share his knowledge, an honour that even the American government that opposed the dissolving communist state recognized as a feat, he knew he had to take up the offer.

However, Austin's arrival in Moscow quickly turned from the Star Trekkian adventures of his first Antarctic expedition to something more like an avante garde psychological thriller mixed with a suspenseful spy espionage film.

Almost immediately after touching down on the tarmac, Austin's luggage disappeared, which contained his wallet, lecture notes on exploring the Antarctic, drawings of proposed modifications for Arctic surveying equipment, and books intended to give as gifts to the Russians. Austin knew that if his luggage got labelled as contraband in this foreign country, his trip would be a short-lived disaster.

Somehow, as if by a Fairy Godmother's nod and a wink, his belongings reappeared (although his wallet, unsurprisingly, no longer had cash inside of it), and Austin had the first signs that this trip would come with its own set of challenges.

When Austin arrived at the Soviet embassy, his collection of books, far from being accepted graciously as an act of friendship, was seen as a suspicious package – some sort of Trojan Horse. Instead, the Soviet government representative interrogated him, screaming, "what are all these books you got in your bags!? What is the secret code? What's all this stuff? What is the message?"

Following a paranoid Cold War narrative, Austin's gift of kinship was, for the Russians, a blatant attempt to smuggle Western propaganda and indoctrination into the Soviet Union. It was a tense introduction to say the least, even though Austin kindly reminded the representative that nothing he had was illicit, saying, "it's all published, you know?"

The trip quickly deteriorated further into a James Bond-esque spy novel. The Soviet government had merged Austin's intelligence files with Austin's deceased Uncle, also named Austin Mardon. "It was stupid because my Uncle was born in the 20s," Austin justifiably complains.

Nonetheless, in a more humorous, Austin Powers-way, this misunderstanding made the Russians believe that Austin was an expert in radar technology – his Uncle's specialty. Once more, to the Russians, Austin looked less like a small-town Albertan geographer, and more like a Cold War secret operative.

Unfortunately, but in hindsight, predictably, Austin never made it to the South Pole with the Soviets, nor lectured at any Russian academies, though they did brief him on the trip he was supposed to take.

Instead, Austin was led on tours through Moscow and never left without a government chaperone. First, he was continuously accompanied by the GRU, then by the KGB. The two groups were adamant that they were not connected to each other, though they both fell under the larger blanket of the USSR government, which didn't dissolve until December of that year.

While Austin was exploring Moscow with his KGB company, he seemed a little too interested in his surroundings, like he was gathering intel for an operation, or so it seemed. Because of Austin's apparently suspicious demeanour, he was incarcerated by the KGB – thrown into a Russian prison.

As we mentioned before, Austin described Russia as the "dark centre of the world," and here, Austin realized that he was in the motionless pitch-black heart of an abysmal prison. The Kraken had swallowed him whole. Austin began his trip hoping to discover a new territory like an explorer finding the Northwest Passage. Unfortunately, the land upon the horizon was a mirage – reflected sun shining off the waters to form a false image. In reality, he headed right to the rocks and sunk like the Titanic in the dark of the night.

Now here is where the reality of the situation is not easy to find. Austin is, nowadays, a schizophrenic, and may have had a psychotic break in Russia, so we must again stress that these are not hard and undeniable facts, but an account of Austin's experience.

Austin was aware during this time that he was losing his grip on reality. Though he didn't guess it was schizophrenia, he knew that the absolute gravity of his situation was dragging his mind into darkness like a star into a black hole. However, he also knew he was a Canadian, sponsored by the Canadian government, and sent to do a task. "I wasn't sure whether I was hallucinating or if it was real. I thought, 'even if I am hallucinating, I should try to keep my wits about me cause I am in Russia,'" details Austin.

There are two incidents in this period of darkness that, true or not, were real for Austin.

First, while under surveillance by the KGB, Austin may have been a victim of an attempted assassination. In one instance, the KGB left him alone for a brief moment and asked him to walk through a door into another room. Afterwards, Austin was sick for days, leaving him to believe it may have been a gas chamber designed to kill him from poisoning or asphyxiation.

Second, Austin may have been drugged by the KGB as a persuasion method to make him sign some unknown documents, though what these documents were, if anything at all, is a matter of speculation.

After these two incidents, Austin's vision was tinged, and he couldn't see yellow. His vision didn't return for days, another sign of a possible poisoning, yet unfortunately, also a sign of a possible psychotic break.

Interpreting these events is like interpreting a Shakespeare text. There are countless possible readings of Austin's experience, but we will never know exactly what all of it means. It is quite possible that Austin was hunted like a lamb in a lion's den by the USSR. It is possible that his mental integrity shattered in Russia, and all the attempted killings were totally hallucinatory. However, like a good literary interpretation, there is likely truth in both interpretations; Austin probably didn't recall the events perfectly, but there is also substantial evidence, specifically Austin's incarceration, to suggest that the Russians were watching him.

Regardless of the reality of these events, Austin was imprisoned and faced a period of darkness until the Canadian embassy sent a Hungarian woman to negotiate his release, or rather, rescue. Austin could not believe that this woman was working for Canada; instead, he thought he was getting tricked once again by some Russians to reveal information. However, the woman gave him a brief relief from his insanity when he told her that "well, I think that... I have a stomach ache."

She responded, "oh, that's indicative of poisoning."

Whether Austin was poisoned physically or not, Austin was sick. Schizophrenia was creeping like a silent killer, disorienting Austin's cognition and propping up like a cobra ready to strike. It seemed that The Canadian Embassy was able to retrieve Austin from Davey Jones' locker, but saving Austin physically would not rescue him from the domineering forces of his brain, which kept his mental health in prison. The leviathan did not let go of Austin's mind.

The Break

"And then, just SNAP, WOW, BANG, CRACK! Everything disintegrates."

Upon returning to Canada, Austin was dismayed to find that none of his professors or colleagues at his South Dakota graduate school believed his recounts of his adventures in Moscow. Although it made a great script for an intellectual thriller, it seemed like pure bologna – at least that's what they told him.

Despite Austin's credentials as an explorer and a published researcher, even his closest relations could not fathom the notion that Russia had selected him to be their first Westerner collaborator since the Cold War – much less that he had been detained by their mythically villainous secret police regiment. Since many of these peers knew Austin's mother had schizophrenia, they figured that he had finally cracked. Ironically, their disbelief would act as a catalyst for what was to come.

Most prominent among these doubting voices was Austin's then-girlfriend, Susan, who did not buy his misadventure for a second. "What are you talking about?" she told him. "Only a bunch of morons would think that an idiot like you knew anything."

While these events had cost Austin his physiological and psychological health, not being believed was but much more distressing for Austin. Austin relates that his experience has given him a window to the trauma rape victims experience when faced with skepticism – the lack of acknowledgement can be harrowing. Says Austin, "it eats into you because you just want to be believed. Then you start thinking, 'did I cause this? Was I a willing participant? Was it my fault?'"

In his desperation to be validated, Austin was confident that he could convince his doubters of specific facts that occurred and alluded to his temporary capture. So, Austin took up the task of recounting his experience in Moscow, resulting in his book, Down and Out and On the Run in Moscow. So great was his desire to be believed that he embarked on the project despite the sobering fear of retaliation from the Russian government. The pros outweighed the cons.

So Austin got to work out of his basement suite north of Edmonton's Whyte Avenue. His living conditions weren't glamorous. In fact, they were anything but. A single dusty lightbulb projected a dusty beam on Austin's few belongings – a small microwave, kettle, and sink. Their shadows cast all around the ratty carpet, which seemed to have absorbed years worth of cigarettes and smoke, judging by the smell. His bedroom, inconspicuously large, contained mostly nothing, except a small table, chair, and bed.

Here, Austin pushed himself to the brink of his first psychotic break over top of his Macintosh Classic. Repeatedly recounting each detail of this traumatic week gnawed at his mental health. It was like exposure therapy, only without the guidance of a professional to administer the treatment in a safe way. He tackled every aspect of the publication by hand, even photocopying as many as 200 copies for the book's first run – all in his dingy abode.

"Writing the book was different from the kind of stress I experienced at graduate school," says Austin. "Going over and over the events during the editorial process and the book production was... pretty bad."

It was one man replaying his Bond movie gone wrong over and over again in a black theatre. It was the book that broke the camel's back.

At the same time, Austin struggled to get a job despite applying 500 times for different positions. In recounting his experience, Austin says, "I have great sympathy for young people. That's the point I cracked at, and my life ended for all intents and purposes. After I became stable in 2006, that's the resounding reason why I started supporting youth in their 20s to amplify their existence rather than just failing and falling under the bus like so many do."

An undercurrent of inner-turmoil was pressurizing during the period Austin spent writing the book while living the post-graduate grind. They were the final months of Austin's old life – a reality that takes on significance for Austin: "They say addicts and alcoholics become stuck at the time they started drinking – and I have noticed this with my schizophrenic friends – they may age, but they are stuck at the age they first became sick. I failed to launch successfully in my late 20s, and have sorta been trapped there," reflects Austin.

But as the tension seemingly climaxed while Austin put words to the final stretch of his Russian misadventure... well, nothing happened.

In fact, things started to ease up. Austin finished his book, and he began to negotiate with the University of South Africa about enrolling for a PhD. He was starting to feel pretty good about himself.

Finally, Austin was getting some traction.

The Bar

As far as university bars go, the library pub was fine – the sort of dingy oasis students flock to for "study nights" that soon unfold into debauchery thanks to generous specials on cheap beer. It was a lowkey Thursday evening in Fall, with perhaps about two dozen people drinking away the sorrows of student life: upcoming midterms, group projects, and 8 am classes.

In the basement, Austin leaned back on a stool against the type of orange-hued wood panelling that was inexplicably popular in the 80s. Across from him sat his childhood friend Larry, who was indulging in a few drinks while Austin opted for some hot camomile tea (a purely financial choice of beverage).

As Larry droned on about something or other, Austin spared him some obligatory eye contact, but his attention belonged to the bar's TV (one of the few light sources in the seedy basement). It showed a National Geographic documentary on colonizing the moon, narrated by Patrick Stewart, who Austin better recognized as Captain Jean-Luc Picard on Star Trek: The Next Generation. As a sci-fi fan and an academic who had many published papers on the moon, Austin found it to be pretty exciting stuff, and his mind began to wander with thoughts and questions about the great beyond.

Larry, seeming to notice Austin's headspace was somewhere else, suggested that Austin take a vacation. Little did Larry know, the vacation had already begun. After hearing Larry out, Austin went up to go to the bathroom. When he returned to his seat, things would be much different.

The girls by the bar dressed in black?

"Oh, they're witches! Witches!" realized Austin.

It seemed like the witches were trying to signal something to him. He figured there must be a symbolic connection between the colour black and the witches' coven. He started recognizing that other bar patrons were in on it, as well.

There was no time to worry about the coven – Austin was swatting at the bees buzzing all around him.

But then the bar's TV started blaring at Austin, projecting images of the moon directly into his mind. The bees didn't seem so important anymore. "Wow, I'm in the moon. The moon is me," thought Austin, encapsulated by the documentary's graphical beauty.

Austin's identification with the documentary began accelerating. It started to take hold in Austin's mind that he could control the video and the direction of Patrick Stewart's narration with his thoughts.

At this point, Austin recalls a fading voice saying, "hello, something is wrong" before giving in to his perception of the reality around him.

Austin began relaying some of these revelations back to Larry – almost screaming to him – about witches, aliens, and travelling to the moon. He told Larry of vampires, werewolves, and how he was afflicted with lycanthropy and vampirism at the same time. He heard werewolves howling at the moon. "It was just bonkers!" says Austin.

Larry, quite taken aback at these imaginative musings, assumed that Austin had taken some LSD while he was in the bathroom. In truth, Larry wasn't far off. In our conversation, Austin explains, "I've never taken LSD, but from what I have read about research in the 60s, taking LSD is very similar to the experience of psychosis."

As far as Larry was concerned, the night was over. Since they only lived a few blocks away from each other, Larry and Austin walked home together under a dreary autumn sky. "You could smell that winter was coming. Everything's dead," Austin adds.

Austin says he didn't get many signals on the walk back (despite talking to himself continuously), but arriving at his dungeon-like basement suite was another story:

Still compelled to share his divine insight, Austin called up his mom, who was in Red Deer, and unloaded on her about his brilliant solutions for Sarajevo, the capital city of Bosnia which had been put under siege after the start of the Yugoslav Wars. After hearing out Austin's suggestion that they send the Serbs "flowers and bombs," which he could then control with his mind, May gestured to Ernest to come over.

"I think Austin's lost it," she said, prompting Ernest to take the phone.

He put his ear to the headset. Moments later, after listening to a sampling of Austin's babbling, Ernest confirmed her suspicions: "yeah, Austin's lost it," he agreed.

They knew that if it wasn't drugs, it was likely schizophrenia, given May's history with the illness. That night, Ernest would leave Red Deer to meet up with Austin and check his mental health.

After ranting away incoherently for an hour to his parents, Austin dialled up his Susan, to spread the good news. Austin gives me his best Susan, saying, "she was like, 'oh really? Oh really? Austin, is something wrong?'"

Susan wasn't equipped for just how 'wrong' things had got.

False Admission
to the Hospital

"All hope abandon, ye who enter here."
Dante Alighieri, The Divine Comedy

Ernest arrived in Edmonton early the next morning. Typically, for most people, Fridays are relaxed days – we wear jeans to work, our colleagues are in humorous moods, and our friends and family are excited for a weekend of sleeping in and taking things slow. Austin, on the other hand, was in for the longest weekend of his life. It would be filled with sombre moods and seriousness, with stress and anxiety, and with time dismantling as if Kronos himself had ripped the hands off the clock.

Upon dawn on a brisk, autumn early morning, Ernest luckily knew to take Austin to the hospital immediately and spared no time driving from Red Deer to the city. Ernest picked up Austin, and sped him to the hospital, hoping to get him proper care for what he already expected would be schizophrenia.

The hospital, in fact, did not initially believe that Austin was experiencing a mental health-related psychosis. Indeed, like medical staff often still do today when faced with psychotic patients, they thought Austin's hallucinations and delusions were drug-induced. Like Larry before them, the staff cast Austin as some guy who took too much LSD, rather than a schizophrenic with a genetic disposition to mental illness.

However, Ernest, and hospital protocol, insisted that they examine Austin for a proper diagnosis. Austin was given antipsychotic medication, an MRI, and put through various tests. After the staff examined him like a wounded alien who crash-landed on Earth, the hospital kept Austin for the day to watch over him, expecting him to sober up. But he never did. Instead, Austin's condition persisted. The clouds around Austin's mind were getting darker, and the storm stretched for an indefinite number of miles, covering his whole mental world.

"The medical staff wanted to give the whole load to my parents," Austin recounts.

So, they told Ernest to take responsibility for his son, thereby lobbing Austin off on his father for what they called "natural support." Yet, Austin later saw, "that's ridiculous. That's like somebody with a broken leg going in and saying, 'oh, your dad can take care of you.'"

The hospital wanted Austin's father to do a professional job. However, Ernest was not a mental health expert. Instead, he lamented, "I can't take care of him. I don't even live in Edmonton. What exactly am I supposed to do? I'm a medievalist."

Peculiarly, Austin, throughout his psychotic break, was not worried. Indeed, he had no reason to worry about himself. "I almost had feelings that I was already dead. Like I died somehow," Austin remarks.

After all, what is there to worry about when the worst, an untimely death, has already happened? For Austin, this was the beginning of a literal death. He was not yet in heaven, nor suffering in hell.

"It felt like purgatory, somewhere on the way there." Austin eerily remarks. "It was like a motif of The Divine Comedy by Dante."

Austin was at the gates of an afterlife, still faced with a quest through the underworld. The medical staff, who "were like interlocutors, like angels, or creatures that were taking care of the dead," decided it was Austin's destiny to traverse a journey through what many may describe as a type of hell. An unmitigated, unsupervised world of psychosis, where reality and falsity equally "just seem like another sensory input."

Ernest was incredibly worried about his son. Having married a schizophrenic, he knew all the attention, time, and difficulty attached to caretaking for someone with the illness. He took his son to the only people he felt could help. That evening, Austin and his father met with a priest at St. Joseph's, a Catholic college within the grounds of the University of Alberta near the hospital.

At the parish, the priest confirmed the message the angels at the hospital had already communicated: that Austin must wander alone. Ernest went into the priest's office to discuss what he must do with Austin.

Austin stared down the hallway of the basilica with his vision kaleidoscoping and zooming to the end of the tunnel. His psychosis still unchecked, he was looking through a telescope of the universe into his future, which his father was deciding carefully behind doors. He watched his father walk solemnly out the doors of the priest's office, side by side with the parishioner.

Ernest returned from the office, walking slowly and solemnly. Then, he spoke to Austin, saying, "the priest told me if I stay here in Edmonton with you, you'll never get the help you need. But if you get admitted today or tomorrow without me, they'll have to take you in because there's no one here to take care of you. The chaplain said I have to leave you to your own devices. You have to find your own way."

Austin had little words to recount to the event, stating, as if he could remember the shock, "my dad was looking very serious. Then... he just abandoned me."

Though Austin was not in the right mind to consider the possible danger of the priest's advice, Ernest knew that there have been cases where people have been taken to emergency and then killed themselves almost right outside the hospital. So it was a risk, a very big risk. However, the priest and Ernest gambled that if Ernest left Austin on his own, the hospital would have to take him in.

Likewise, the priest also informed Austin that he would not take Austin into the church for the time being. So, the council had spoken, and the hospital, the church, and Austin's father all refused to take him in. Indeed, contrary to a schizophrenic hallucination, Austin's life became comparable to a page torn from The Divine Comedy. Austin had to make a journey by himself, with no Virgil to guide him. He was on his own.

Wandering in the Descent of My Insanity

"Many Schizophrenics pass most of their time neither on earth, nor in heaven, nor even hell, but in a gray, shadowy world of phantoms and unrealities."
- Aldous Huxley, Heaven and Hell

One could easily sum up Austin's next 24 hours in a few sentences. The hospital, the church, and Austin's father left him to his devices. Austin wandered the streets of Edmonton for a day. He stumbled into another church, one where the pastor did not know him. Even so, the pastor saw that Austin was suffering from a mental illness of some sort, and took him to the hospital, which could not deny him service this time.

However, although Austin often nonchalantly describes his psychotic wandering this way, maybe to spare a student fear or to avoid detailing the long, convoluted story, his experience was far from trivial. Even picturing such an experience can cause fear in someone with a strong enough imagination. There was a great risk in leaving Austin unsupervised – he could wander into traffic, he could kill himself, he could get arrested, he could get robbed or assaulted, or he could even scare himself with his hallucinations like a bad trip, to name a few of the possible dangers. Nonetheless, Austin was alone.

The rest of Austin's freaky Friday, and the evening that followed, are a blur. Austin disappeared, becoming a ghost in the night's shadow, led by his hallucinations wherever they beckoned him. By the morning, Ernest was quite concerned for Austin – he had hoped that after an evening of walking around Edmonton, someone would have helped Austin find his way to the hospital. To Ernest's despair, he could not contact anyone who knew where Austin was. The hospitals across the city, Austin's friends, and the church members were all unaware of Austin's whereabouts.

It was an overcast morning, neither bursting with colours illuminated by the sun nor covered in black clouds pouring rain and gloom onto the earth. No, the sky was gray. Similarly, Austin did not feel like he was facing the gates of heaven or trapped in the plains of hell. Instead, as we mentioned, Austin was seeing the world as a symbolic purgatory, and, if only by chance, the setting of this scene fit Austin's experience neatly.

One of Austin's first experiences on this strange day occurred when he was aimlessly trudging around the university area. Across the street from the hospital nearby, he saw a familiar face: Susan. He silently approached her, hoping to hold on to some modicum of stability as things were falling apart. Susan squashed that idea, telling him they could not stay together because of his illness. Just like that, Austin was left alone, confused, shocked, and psychotic.

"All the sudden, I was hit with lightning bolts and heard angelic voices and lights shattering. I said, 'my god, my life is over.' That was when I was really psychotic," Austin says.

Strikes of lightning thrown from Zeus' fingertips erupted the world into dazzling sparkles glittering against the sun's rays. Austin was experiencing psychosis before, but this was a new level of madness as a new solitary universe sucked him into its gravitational pull. He could recognize things around him, but none of them looked, felt, or meant the same as they had before. His surroundings became an infinite spring of symbols brimming with inexhaustible significance.

The symbolic aspects of Austin's psychosis were likely an effect of his preconceived notions. As a firm believer in Christianity and, especially, thanks to his father, the medieval specialist, Austin had knowledge of the symbols associated with his religion. We cannot say exactly what all of Austin's experiences meant to him, but we can briefly look at some of the things he found symbolic.

After leaving his home in the University area, Austin felt he needed to climb into a manhole for one reason or another. Looking back at his strange destination, Austin says, "I felt I had died and I had to go into the grave. Or something strange like that."
In keeping with Austin's feeling of a death, it seems he might have been searching for a final resting place, and luckily, he never found his way into any manholes.

Austin saw garbage strewn along the street as if it was a coded message, finding secret meaning in everything. He was talking to himself, although people passing by, especially those in the university area, didn't seem to think much of it since it was not abnormal to see a professor wandering the streets talking to themselves in that part of the city.

Austin's visions were likely a symptom of his consciousness since, even when we don't have a mental illness, part of our consciousness is always putting symbolism on the whole world. "It's not surprising that when you get sick, our projections get ratcheted up and come out in strange ways," Austin notes. "That's why schizophrenics come up with new ideas – because they see things differently."

Sadly, Austin's visions were beyond control and indiscernible from reality, so he wouldn't be coming up with any novel inventions.

Whether guided by fate, projections of his consciousness, or mere chance, Austin wandered from the University area of Edmonton to its Southside borders, which was a total of about 15 miles. He was experiencing some sort of struggle – a journey with a feeling of "grandeur." It would be remiss to brush off Austin as just another 'crazy person' overemphasizing hallucinations and delusions. That is to say, we can't overlook Austin's experience as trivial. If faced with the same circumstances, any sober-minded or mentally strong person would feel the intensity and risk of abandonment by their beacons of trust.

Austin spent lots of time praying, and he tells us with a giggle under his breath, "I prayed a lot, but I don't know if God listens to schizophrenics cause usually it's just crazy prayers."

This near heartbreaking statement shows that even if Austin was not in the right mind to handle his experiences alone, he was aware that he was going through something serious.

Austin's journey through a part-hallucination, part real, mythical experience took him throughout the evening. Again, he felt an identity with creatures of the night: mainly werewolves and vampires. He found himself howling at the moon, which was glowing and illuminating a world of phantoms and unrealities amidst the backdrop of a midnight sky. Austin's walk through the pages of a vampiristic European folktale lasted the whole evening, and before he knew it, the dawn of the Saturday sun was arising. The horizon beaconed with a new light, sending Austin in a new direction.

Again, his personality or beliefs could have directed him specifically, but as if the interlocutors of the afterlife were leading him, or God had indeed heard his prayers, Austin's journey landed him on the front doors of a

church he had never visited. Around 4 or 5 O'clock am, after roaming the Edmonton streets for a full rotation of the Earth, like a convert at the feet of Christ, he crawled up the stairs of a St. Andrew's Catholic church and made his way inside. All he can say about the situation is that "I thought I knew it was a friendly place. When I entered the church, I said something like: 'where's God?'"

He may not have gotten his one-on-one with God directly, but he spoke to the usher at this church who could quickly infer that Austin was mentally ill. Not knowing the medical staff had kicked Austin out less than 24 hours before, the usher drove Austin back to the hospital.

Just like that, Austin had returned from whence he came. Yet, this time things were different. Austin was alone, his father nowhere to be found, and therefore, the hospital couldn't pawn him off onto his "natural supports." This time, they had to take him in.

Overall, Austin simply states, "it was a very spiritual experience."

Austin doesn't mean spiritual only in some sensational sense of a wild LSD trip. Instead, Austin thinks that spirituality is more like regular life – the regular reality. It is precisely because Austin went through an unimaginably life-changing few days, days that were sobering and dangerous in a very real sense, that "it was a very spiritual experience…"

Now, the hospital couldn't bounce Austin like someone in some sort of drug-induced haze or disregard him and lock him up in an isolation room for a few hours as if he had a bad trip. Austin's return to the hospital would be an equally momentous experience because it signalled the first signs of him getting better. It was the first step in Austin's return from purgatory to the reality of the human world.

To the ER, and Beyond

"I can feel it. I can feel it. My mind is going. There is no question about it. I can feel it"
HAL-9000, 2001: A Space Odyssey

The St. Andrew's usher rushed Austin to the ER. The hospital put Austin in a different section than his first visit. When Austin made his return to the hospital, he was babbling gibberish about wolves and vampires, still afterglowing from his folktale journey the evening before, and could hardly talk to the medical staff. "I probably sounded like I was on a bad roofie trip or something," remarks Austin.

As was common at the time, the doctors, once again, simply assumed that Austin was on drugs (it was around the first semester for University students, after all).

"So that's the first thing they do is assume you're on drugs," Austin explains. "The next thing they do is take a blood sample, and then they detox you. They scan everything in your blood. Just everything. They can find thyroid problems, cancer – anything."

During these tests, Austin was still hallucinating, and so he couldn't quite wrap his head around the situation. "I thought, 'wow, this is funky,'" Austin recalls. "I kept thinking it was like a Stanley Kubrick film, like 2001: A Space Odyssey."

It's not surprising that Austin's experience felt like a trippy, uncomfortable sci-fi thriller. Most people would feel that an experience like Austin's, filled with hallucinations of religious symbolism and folklore creatures in the streets, churches, and modern hospitals of a 20th-century Canadian city, could only be the work of a film genius taking them for a dramatic ride.

Following the religious sci-fi theme, Austin says, "I felt like I was being electrocuted in the emergency department... I thought, 'Wow, this is like being crucified.'"

Austin was going through an execution – he was on the longest green mile headed toward crucifixion on an electric chair. Thomas Kempis, a famous Catholic theologian, tells believers, "we ought to deny ourselves and imitate Christ through bearing the cross" (The Imitation of Christ), but Austin's hallucinations were too literal an interpretation of this adage.

According to Austin, the last time he was in the ER, he was mostly like a zombie. This time, he was experiencing "various light shows" and was "actually shaking." Austin was incoherent during his first encounter with the ER, but here he was electrified.

The searches for an easy diagnosis, such as drugs, came up short. The medical staff were stumped, and worse, knew that whatever was wrong with Austin was likely a serious mental illness – something that he wouldn't sober up from with some patient waiting. A few hours after Austin's initial arrival, medical staff placed Austin in a yellow chair and wheeled him up to the hospital's fourth floor – the psych ward. Though he wasn't sober-minded, the reality of his situation still began to sink in quickly.

"The moment I crossed the threshold of the psych ward, I started bawling and crying," says Austin. He continues, "I experienced a brief moment of lucidity. I realized all of my expectations to be an astronaut, to get a PhD, and be married with a child and dog and have a home... I knew I was going to be homeless. I'd never write anything again."

Like the ultimate reveal of a mystery murder novel, or a heartbreaking turn at the end of a Shakespearean tragedy, Austin, who was both the protagonist and the audience at the same time, saw the end of his story unfold before his eyes. Meanwhile, the nurses dragging Austin around were mumbling to each other "oh, he's being psychotic."

He continues, "at that moment, it just hit me. I said, 'my god, this is the end.' I could have been very suicidal at that point, and I probably was because it all overwhelmed me. The label itself is so terrible and so demeaning – a lot of people would rather die than acknowledge they have it."

"Is that something you remember feeling in that moment?" I ask.

"Yeah I felt suicidal," Austin admits. "My life was over. I felt it wasn't worth living anymore. It's like if you lost 50 IQ points right now, what would happen?"

Scholars have said that the rate of suicide in individuals with schizophrenia doubles within the first five years of their disagnoses. Austin's father, Ernest, knew this tragic outcome was a serious possibility the first time Austin went to the ER, and Austin wasn't blind to this risk either. As Austin said, he felt that his life had ended.

This feeling wasn't a delusion either, he felt his life was over because he was deluded and hallucinating. There was no grandiose symbology projecting from his unconscious that his psychosis was making him see. No, his world had, in a real sense, collapsed in front of him. "I tried to avoid this struggle with schizophrenia," he says. "This avoidance was a combination of 25 years of being with my mother and her schizophrenia, so I knew totally what it meant, maybe even more than the doctors."

Accompanied by three nurses, Austin was rolled to a locked-down unit deep in the bowels of the ward. There, he 'waited.' "As a patient, you wait," explains Austin.

He recounts lapsing in and out of consciousness for days. After awakening more indefinitely, he was prescribed Haloperidol, which Austin says made him shuffle around like Frankenstein – the "Haloperidol Shuffle" as he calls it. This was Austin's first foray into the world of antipsychotics and neuroleptics, which lasts to this day.

Austin needed to relearn how to function under the drug's influence – a lesson that would prove herculean in its magnitude. He recalls being mentally incapacitated as if he were a four-year-old child. I asked him to recall his first impression of the drugs, but before I could finish speaking, he cut me off; "it's like being hit with a truck."

I didn't know how to proceed – Austin is usually more comprehensive, embellishing his analogies with colour and context. I muttered "okay," hoping to cue elaboration, but Austin remained curt, saying, "If you gave a normal person an antipsychotic, it would be like taking a sledgehammer or baseball bat and whacking them in the side of the head."

Perhaps that's all there is to say about such an experience.

Austin's deflated spirit was met by a vicious absence of hope, forcing his affect and outlook into nosedive. He says that, while only on the ward for a handful of months, it took years before he felt hopeful about his life again – "years, years later" he chants.

Austin's then-psychiatrist told him to retire his pursuits in favour of a nominal, unextraordinary life.

"I'm afraid that symptoms like mine got thrown under the rug because they were focused on illnesses like depression, which are more straightforward to cure," Austin reflects. "It's like, if you're injured in battle and have a mortal injury, they put you aside and give you enough morphine to die – that was comparable to schizophrenia. Whereas with depression, they could fix you up more quickly and get you back onto the field. With schizophrenia, it was, like, intense – like a head wound, like a full-body cavity wound. Serious. Years of recovery."

In the wake of grappling with crippling disequity, Austin turned flippant and refused to take his meds. He was miserable.

He stood at a juncture: Rebel against the forces that served to save – and waste him, or continue to roll with the punches that had him hogtied. Austin appeared to have his mind made. He was going to fight. If not for a fateful visit, he might still be skirmishing for the win.

My Father's First Visit

"But life is full of Hard Choices / And risk is part of the game / Be brave, ignore
doubting voices / make the choice, life won't be the same."
Jojoba Mansell, Hard Choices

At last, Ernest had caught wind that Austin had been admitted to the hospital at the University of Alberta, and yet again, he sped over to the hospital as fast as he could, unannounced.

It had been days since he had last seen Austin, and it churned his stomach into knots, oozing with pings of nausea and gut feelings of emptiness. Leaving Austin alone was the hardest thing he had ever done. Every excruciating, anxiety-riddled moment had been an opportunity for Ernest to despair in his lack of foresight with Austin growing up. In retrospect, his willingness to overlook Austin's prodromal symptoms was all too clear.

"He blamed himself – that he never protected me enough when I was a young kid," recalls Austin. "That's what a lot of parents do when they get disabled kids. They blame themselves."

Evidently, Austin and Ernest had a complicated father-son relationship. According to Austin, medievalists tend to be strange to begin with, and Ernest's marriage with a person with schizophrenia had only developed his most eccentric personality traits and behavioural quirks. Beyond that, Austin postures that Ernest had a limited amount of energy that he spent attending to his wife rather than his kids.

Yet despite these complications, Austin did have a unique connection with his dad: academics. Austin admits that, growing up, he had no real affinity or passion for academics – at least, at first. The true reason Austin chose to pursue them was in hopes of earning his father's approval. It worked, drawing the two closer together, and soon, Austin was preparing to carry on his father's legacy. In turn, Ernest did what he could to nurture his son's career. As an undergrad, Austin began working with his father, helping him to write books and publish articles.

While the foundation of their professional relationship was built on a false pretense in regards to Austin's true interests, it did lead to true companionship and understanding between the two. In this way, it was something to treasure, and even more, something to miss.

This tragedy was not lost on Ernest as he entered Austin's hospital room – the slipping away of his professional legacy, expectations, and, more importantly, connection with his son. "It's like one of your kids got a terminal illness, except they're going to be alive for 50 years," Austin elaborates.

Many times, Austin had felt as though he were dead, but seeing the same revelation unfold on his father's face was hellish. Initially, the surprise of his father from behind the curtain was a much-needed jolt of familiarity in what had been a bender of strangeness. But Austin knew his father, and he could see the sorrow in his moistened eyes, and how the worry had carved creases and crinkles in his brow. The surprise dissipated, leaving Austin with emotional numbness in its stead. He sunk into his bed – his throat too seized to make a sound.

Ernest checked himself, recognizing that Austin had caught a glimpse of his vulnerability, and how it had punctured his soul. He forced a more comforting disposition and attempted to cheer Austin up by talking about his accomplishments in school and Antarctica – pathos, to what was now the old days.

As the conversation waned thin, Ernest took a deep breath, preparing to reveal the true intention behind his visit. "The doctors say you're refusing to take any meds," said Ernest.

Austin shook his head, saying, "I don't want pills, dad."

"Do you want to repeat your mother's chaotic life?" Ernest fired back. "If you want to have a better life than your mother, then this is what you have to do."

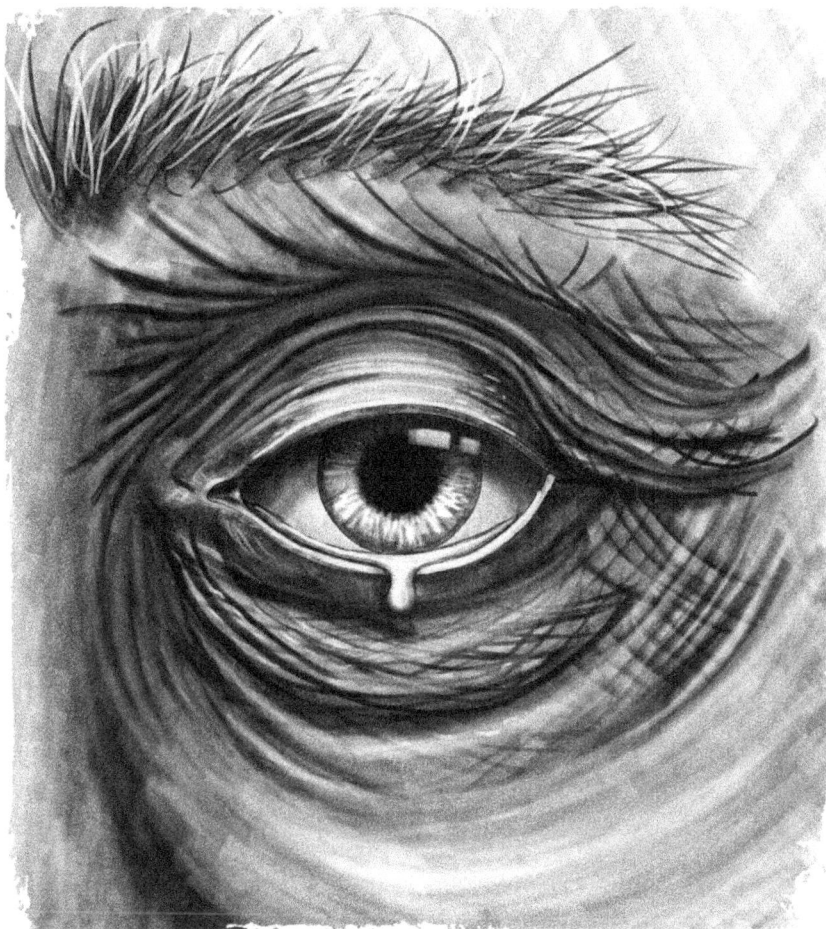

It may have been the most honest thing Ernest ever said about his wife's condition. Austin thought back to his childhood, recalling the pain and hurt that had arisen between him and his siblings because of their mother's illness and her lack of cooperation.

"I don't wanna do that," Austin reluctantly confessed.

Ernest continued, "I know it's not a great option. It's close to being the worst. But it's not. Sitting like this and doing nothing is. So you can either lose or lose even more. You have to try to take the best of the worst choices."

They both knew about the side effects of the medication and what it meant – the heavy sedation, the drooling, the stigma. In the early 90s, the only treatment for schizophrenia was essentially to sedate to the point of eradicating any symptoms, often leaving the person a "zombie" of their former selves.

Ernest didn't relent. After all, the other option was to be institutionalized. Or homeless."You just have to take them, and hopefully, they'll improve over time. Maybe one day, we could even publish together again," he told Austin.

It wasn't good news, but it was the closest thing to hope Austin had felt in a long time. "Okay," he eked.

Ernest couldn't have anticipated it, but he was right about the meds. They have improved dramatically in modern times, returning Austin his cognition and allowing him to live what he calls a "semi-normal" life.

Meanwhile, the doctors were shocked that after just a three and a half-hour-long visit, Ernest had completely reversed Austin's aversion to medication, and quite possibly, the trajectory of Austin's entire life. "I think sometimes an early decision or a course of action in a new world could have dramatic effects down the road," says Austin. "It can set the pattern. Small changes, especially in a new world, can really have an impact cause it keeps expanding the further it goes out."

A small change, but its significance cannot be understated. Now, taking meds is a central tenet of Austin's philosophy. He relates, "I think God wants us to be happy and healthy, and if possible, live our destinies and try to have a good life. In the context of 27 years, the impact I've made by making this decision and telling people about it has been monumental. It's changed a whole group of people that otherwise might have fallen aside, so it's impacted a lot more people than just me."

Without his father's intervention, Austin acknowledges that he may have well-entrenched himself in his opposition to meds, relegating himself to the shadowy realm of his distorted mind. For Austin, it highlights the importance of taking good counsel, trust, and staying with a direction when you fall aside. "Those were dark days," he says. "There was no hope. But I just put one foot in front of the other until there was hope."

Many steps would still need to be taken.

Boredom – Months Of

"Life swings like a pendulum backward and forward between pain and boredom."
Arthur Schopenhauer, World as Will and Representation

A motionless and slack-jawed Austin hunched over his window overlooking the roof of the hospital's foyer about two floors down. There, lay a very dead bird. Dormant, he stared at it. Minutes turned into hours. Time moved like a moth in molasses. The hands of the clock slowly waved second by second like the air was made of sludge.

Look, psych wards are not exactly known for their many luxuries or entertainment. Mostly, they are incredibly dull and uneventful. Austin elaborates, "we'd have plenty of time to stare into space, or watch TV, or go to therapy. Psych wards are pure boredom. You might die of boredom rather than anything else."

Everyone is a hero in their own story, and in Austin's tale, the hero became human. Even worse, he went from an archetype of exploration, triumph, and beating the odds to an archetype of isolation, loss, monotony, and tragedy. The dragon slayer was in the belly of the beast.

Initially, Austin wanted to read, but due to his new medication, he could barely process 10 words at a time – a far cry from the days when he would put 700-page books like 7 Pillars of Wisdom by Lawrence of Arabia away in a single sitting. He couldn't even catch Star Trek: The Next Generation because he was outnumbered by legions of female patients who preferred to watch "reality TV shows about bulimia." Austin says that boredom is soul-killer, and thus, it did not take long for him to put on a considerable amount of weight and slip further into the throes of depression. All of his dreams and hobbies were lost.

And so, Austin found himself with nothing better to do than gawk at the avian casualty, who's life probably came to an end when it smashed into the very window Austin had been fogging up with his breath for the past several hours.

"That's like me," thought Austin. "This bird is dead. My life is dead. Everything's over, and nothing's gonna happen."

It seemed as though any semblance of hope Ernest had inspired within Austin was washed away by a flood of side effects and lethargy. He was as directionless as the Israelites who wandered the deserts for 40 years.

Unlike the Israelites, Austin never got sick of the food. "I thought it was great, but everyone else complained about it," says Austin. "I remember having this one meeting with all the patients and nurses so they could take our complaints. Everybody was complaining about the food, and I said, 'no, it's great food,' and everybody looked at me like I was an idiot."

Low food standards aside, Austin got along with the other patients well enough, as they had plenty of time to talk and become acquainted. Socializing, after all, was really the only compelling form of entertainment... that, and people-watching. "For excitement, I'd go into the central area in the middle of the four pods and watch them go in and out of the smoke room," explains Austin.

High-brow stuff.

When we are bored, the most minute activities and achievements become monumental. For Austin, the humdrum of the hospital was broken up by the occasional visit from family. Perhaps Austin's favourite memory came during one of his dad's subsequent visits. According to Austin, he was babbling to the nurse about 'how great penguins were' and his expedition to Antarctica (which she did not believe happened), when Ernest walked in the room and caught wind of the conversation. Ernest agreed with Austin, saying, "yeah, they're a great creature. In the medieval and renaissance worlds, they were considered Christlike because they pecked their own breasts so their chicks could drink the blood. You know, how like we drink the blood of Christ."

The nurse, apparently not a Catholic, ruffled her papers and left the room, disturbed from the morbid twist of ornithological conversation.

Austin also had some interesting encounters with his mom at this time. In some sense, it brought them closer together, as May could give Austin advice on how to 'survive the mental ward.' She was even able to convince the hospital staff to switch his medication, so he could avoid debilitating constipation – much to the literal relief of Austin's belaboured gastrointestinal tract.

Austin recalls another visit in which he proudly presented his mother with a tiny car with wheels on it that he made in a recreational therapy class. Thinking back to his mother's patronizing reactions, Austin recounts, "she said, 'ooh okay, that's nice.' It was like something a two-year-old would call stupid, but it was the only thing I could do, and I was very impressed with it."

Not all the family visits were so ideal. For instance, Austin's sister reamed him out for ending up in the hospital. Regarding her hostility, Austin says, "I think she always felt I was doing this on purpose… trying to get attention from the family. She got mad at me when I went to Antarctica as well."

Unfortunately, as typical as it is for parents to blame themselves for their children's illnesses (as Ernest did), it is also not uncommon to assign blame to the sick person themselves. A lifetime of context can cause rather unfortunate distortions on the way people perceive their sick family members. Austin explains that this effect is part of the reason couples often divorce after one of them incurs a severe permanent disability.

Strikingly, the most significant advice didn't come from Austin's family or even his friends. Instead, it was his occupational therapist. One class, Austin was lamenting that he was no longer capable of activities that could make any money. In turn, she suggested that once he was out of the hospital, he could volunteer. Austin didn't mind that idea one bit – he wanted, so badly, to be needed.

It was the beginning of a new dream for Austin – one that would see his life become about service rather than personal gain. "It was different from my old dream, which was all science and very mechanistic," explains Austin. "This dream was more emotional, which was a side of myself I had completely ignored. It was about living and contributing."

In our dreams, things just happen – everything works. However, in reality, if we are to achieve even a semblance of our dreams, we must work, fail, and continue to try until we succeed, and that success only comes if we are lucky. Austin would soon find his eagerness alone would not prepare him to live on his own. After leaving the hospital, his life was going to be more difficult than even he was capable of imagining.

Trials by, Trails of Fire

"From there we came outside and saw the stars."
Dante Alighieri, The Divine Comedy

If the church, the hospital, and Ernest hadn't left Austin to wander in the descent of his insanity, Ernest would have had no choice but to take care of Austin. If Ernest had taken care of Austin on his own without getting Austin a proper diagnosis and treatment, Austin may never have gotten the medications necessary to help him recover to a point where he could take another stab at life. His time spent wandering was a trial by fire, crackling with the fiery coals of his hallucinations as Austin meandered back to the hospital.

In spite of the hazards, Austin had passed this examination, relentlessly asserting his diligence and integrity all the way through. The trial by fire led Austin back to the hospital, which was its own adventure filled with challenges of accepting his fate, coming to terms with his illness, and facing monotony and boredom for months on end.

Now, Austin's wrists were draped with privileges for his good behaviour and trustworthy temperament. They may have been just bracelets to the hospital staff, but to Austin, they were artifacts accumulated throughout his odyssey – talismans that signalled to the guard he was ready to move on with his quest.

As the interlocutors escorted Austin into his chariot, they laid a luminous white bag on his lap, full of the worldly possessions he had accumulated throughout several months of purgatory. They guided him through the narrow corridors of the labyrinth and rounded one final corner, bringing the sealed Gates of Heaven into view. As Austin approached, the towering doors flung open, pulling in a bright winter wind that felt cool on his face.

Austin stood up and took his first step outside, graduating from his trial of fire.

"I was excited, I was very excited," Austin exclaims.

However, he was now faced with a new trial: Building the entirety of his life from the ground up. Like a city after a war, Dresden or Nagasaki, Austin's past life was totally demolished by the bombings and scorched earth policies of schizophrenia.

But Austin was hopeful – he had his new dream, and he was sure he could accomplish it. Sure, his life would be much different from the one he had before, but at least it was a life.

Unfortunately, even this new normal was not going to be so simple, and Austin was not prepared for the difficulty and strain that was to come.

Upon exiting the hospital, Austin was met by May, and they prepared themselves for the frozen walk home. Even though it was only five blocks away, Austin struggled like a wounded soldier on a fog-ridden battlefield. His limited mobility, caused by his frostbitten feet, combined with dizzy disorientation from his medication, made him nearly slip on the ice multiple times. Though he wished to be back on his feet, he simply couldn't get on his feet at all. Though he was determined to get back to his regular life, he, unfortunately, was in for a rude awakening.

The first few months were a struggle. During the first week back home, Austin's medicine caused him to freeze up and convulse. Luckily, his parents came up every weekend to help out Austin however they could. In particular, May helped Austin to navigate the bleak world of early antipsychotic medication and such side effects. "The doctors never talked about it cause they don't care about the side effects," Austin explains.

There was a certain irony to May's helpfulness when it came to medication. "Even though she wouldn't take them, she wanted me to," says Austin with a giggle. "She thinks she is the sane one. She is willing to admit that I'm crazy, but not that she's crazy."

But after his parents left on Sunday night, Austin would have a pit in his stomach, bracing for another week of helplessness and, even more distressing, loneliness.

What Austin couldn't have known was that his trial by fire wasn't the only problem he faced; there was also the trail of fire left behind in the wake of his illness. As is a common issue for those struggling with mental illness, many of Austin's old friends, colleagues, and family left him behind – they ostracized Austin due to his mental illness, corrupted by the stigma of schizophrenia. He was dead to them. "A lot of them were grieving; a lot of people grieved when I got sick. It was very odd," Austin recalls.

Austin is right – upon examination, this response is quite strange. After all, we tend to grieve when people die, not when they become sick. Unfortunately, Austin was, and maybe today still is, dead for many people.

Susan broke up with him, telling him straightforwardly: "I can't be with you because you're sick." Ernest, Austin's said that his father "blamed himself, he thought 'this caused it, that caused it.'"

Whatever the case, his old friends and colleagues no longer paid him much mind. "Before my schizophrenia, I had a decent-sized circle of friends. But it was slowly shrinking because when you're poor, you lose social capital," says Austin.

Austin concedes that the loss of his friends was more a process of drifting away then an act of cutting off, they weren't cruel. Regardless of whether his friends were intentionally malicious, the new poor and mentally ill Austin was no longer in their lives. As if their friend Austin was dead and relegated to a distant memory, they moved on.

So, Austin would try to go out for coffee whenever possible (which remains to this day, his favourite pastime) just to be around other human beings. However, his medication would cause him to space out and sit still "like a vegetable." In turn, cafe patrons would stare or ask if he was okay – interactions that fell eons short of the connection he so sorely missed. Austin was a ghost of his former self, limping and lagging behind his own shadow.

Austin's experience with the academics in his life followed the same pattern. Austin wanted to go back to the University of Texas for a PhD, but after he achieved his Master's, he says, "they'd washed their hands of me."

Universities would not want to take in someone who had a mental illness, and they definitely wouldn't recognize a former graduate who they now considered crazy. "I think they were shocked and mortified because a lot of intellectuals were afraid of going insane themselves," Austin pontificates. "So, it was like a mirror to them saying, 'I could go there myself.' A lot of people were scared, my illness scares them because they think, 'Oh my God, if Austin can go insane after going to Moscow, Antarctica, and writing articles, then what chance do I have?'"

As if by a work of a divine prankster, Austin's relationship to the church resembled the same malignant motif, and the friendship between them went up in flames. "One priest said that he wouldn't talk to me. He said I talked too much," Austin reflects.

Because this priest would no longer speak to Austin, as if Austin was a babbling toddler who needed to learn respect, Austin inevitably switched churches, forced into a different avenue to pursue his faith.

To put a final touch on Austin's trail of fire, the destruction in his life caused by the labelling and stigma surrounding him, Austin had no luck finding a "normal person" job. Trauma had wrung Austin's mind free of the motor and cognitive skills required to do many basic tasks around the house. On several occasions, Austin remembers the embarrassment he felt when he just couldn't figure out how to cook macaroni and cheese. But the reality was that something as simple as boiling water was once again a brand new skill he had to learn all over. Instead, as if he was still sitting desolate and alone in the psych ward, he just opted for sandwiches and more coffee runs.

Without the ability to perform the simplest of tasks, work was even further out of the question, and not just because of his schizophrenia. Further complicating the matter was his souvenir from Antarctica – the permanent frostbite in his feet. "I was falling down a lot," Austin details. "I thought, 'I can't get a physical job, like a construction job, because I might fall and hurt myself.'"

Unfortunately, people, including potential employers, were unable to see beyond his mental illness and thought even his physical disabilities were schizophrenia symptoms. As he said, "a lot of people just see the schizophrenia, but I have frozen lungs, frozen hands, and frozen feet."

Given the insurmountable sum of his physical disabilities, Austin thought he would have a better chance trying to write and publish his dad's incomplete work from his old life. That didn't go well either. Years later, Austin looked back on some of the articles he was trying to write during the time and found they were utterly incoherent. These rudimentary skills that he had been able to do his whole life were gone. Austin had passed through

the River of Lethe, his memory washed away – burnt up and scattered like ash in the wind.

His difficulties weren't even regulated to chores and work activities. Even watching television became difficult. If it was too complex or required you to pay a lot of attention to the plotline, Austin couldn't follow along. "My favourite show became Married with Children," Austin notes. "It was the only thing I could understand at that point."

The salience of Austin's cognitive and physical disabilities made it easy for the people in Austin's life to see him as someone different. The fire of labelling allowed people to pathologize him – to think that he had become the illness. Sadly, many others with mental illness follow their labels and identify with their illness. "Sometimes it's the coping mechanism a person does to themselves because they have to come to terms with this new social, physical, and mental environment," Austin muses. "But I refused to become my illness or be labelled as a monster."

Even today, Austin's trail of fire has not smouldered out, and it has the potential to flare up and engulf things from time to time. He relapsed in 1995 for about 10 days, disregarding his medications and falling back into his psychosis while travelling overseas, though he luckily got back onto his meds. Further, the students he hires often cast judgments on his schizophrenia or stigmatize him as someone to be pitied, not to mention the countless government officials, university affiliates, doctors, and politicians he deals with daily. The flames catch up when Austin is trying to deliver a speech or submit paperwork for a grant and his communicative or cognitive abilities short-circuit. Thankfully, his students, close friends, and, most of all, his wife, Catherine, are always there to double-check his paperwork or give him (literal) reality checks.

Although the world Austin knew was disappearing before him because of the trail of fire consuming almost every aspect of his life like a vicious wildfire, he was not about to let himself burn up. Like Lot turning away from the fire and brimstone consuming Sodom, Austin had no choice but to journey into an "undiscovered country" and search for a new world to call home. He was about to face a new trial by fire, a test of his abilities under immense pressure coming from all sides: from his family, his society, his doctors, and most importantly, himself.

The Rebirth of My Old Life

"You will burn and you will burn out; you will be healed and come back again."
Fyodor Dostoevsky, The Brothers Karamazov

Despite Austin's best efforts to return to some semblance of familiarity, he seemed to be disembarking fully from the life he used to have, drifting through vast, stormy oceans and facing crashing tidal waves with a broken compass.

But then, the winds shifted.

At this point in our interviews with Austin, we were taken with how suddenly his tone shifted from the morose of recalling his existential despair and hopelessness to animated excitement. That's how rapidly the best parts of his old life returned to him, and the seeds of a new life were planted. Two specific events during his transition in life allowed for this resurrection:

The first came during Austin's new found life in volunteering. Initially, after his release from the hospital, Austin was deeply distressed about how he would survive without skills and the ability to make money. Austin's family physician, Dr. Rosenstock, had him fill out some forms that he couldn't quite understand given the cognitive obstacles he was facing. It made for quite the shock when, several weeks later, Rosenstock said, "you now have guaranteed income for the rest of your life."

Turns out, Dr. Rosenstock had submitted Austin's application for the Albertan Government's Assured Income for the Severely-Handicapped (AISH) program, which, at long last, gave Austin the flexibility to pursue his occupational therapist's advice and volunteer. It was his first foray into his new dream.

And so, four months after his hospital discharge, Austin set sail for the Schizophrenia Society in Edmonton. There, he would stuff envelopes for an hour and a half a day. A simple task for some, but a milestone for Austin, who had internally cast himself as "useless" since he started taking his medication. Austin remembers, "I felt like I did something. I did envelopes for an hour and a half. Everybody had been telling me to just sit around and drink coffee for the rest of my life, but I did something."

This small victory had monumental implications: it restored Austin's confidence in himself – the confidence necessary to steer his destiny away from the solitary life he was beginning to believe was fate. He was a capable person. Later that month, Austin gave the first public speech on schizophrenia for the Schizophrenia Society at the old Charles Camsell Hospital. Even with Austin's slurred speech and the drool leaking from his lip's corner, the audience was captivated by his insights. It was another feather in a cap that desperately needed plumage, and Austin wanted more.

Austin was motivated to push forward and other groups for which he could volunteer. He found other organizations, such as the Prosper Place Clubhouse and Unsung Heroes – a peer support group for people with schizophrenia. Austin quite enjoyed going. "People would introduce themselves, and we would get a speaker. After, we'd go for a coffee afterwards," Austin reflects fondly.

Opportunity knocked when the organization found itself in desperate need of leadership. As a result, Austin remarks that he was "dragooned in," and that the new role was a really big deal for him. Set on expanding the organization's reach, Austin made concerted efforts to develop relationships with the community and other non-profits. He gushes of the talent he was able to procure for speeches and Q&A events, saying, "I really put in a lot of effort into it. I got assistant deputy ministers, I got ministers, I got people from the government, I got politicians, I got priests."

Through Unsung Heroes, Austin was able to bring circulation to his slumbering confidence, resourcefulness, and ability to operate. He remains a chairman of the organization to this day.

The second event was in 1996, when the doctors were able to change his medication to Risperidone. "They talk about the 90s being the 'decade of the brain,'" reflects Austin. "There were all these advances with our understanding of the brain."

The significance of this medication shift wasn't immediately clear to Austin. His epiphany would come two days later at the University of Alberta library, during Austin's attempt to find the books he had published before his psychotic break. It wasn't the first time he had tried to do so – not even close – but his low-functioning cognition kept him from succeeding.

Eerie thoughts were beginning to creep in Austin's mind, questioning if he ever wrote the books in the first place – that they were just more delusions. After all, nobody else believed that Austin's books were real. "Dennis Anderson, a former Cabinet Minister, became a great friend. But the first time he met me, he thought I had, like, about a 50 IQ," Austin recalls, giggling. "I was trying to explain to him I wrote a book on Alberta politics. 'You're in it, Dennis.' And he just thought I was nuts. Like, who's this drooling guy?"

Initially, it seemed liked Dennis was right. Austin's search wasn't going well. He had forgotten how to use the computer catalogue and was too embarrassed to ask for help. But after spending yet another day pouring through stacks of books, he pulled a familiar cover from a stack of literature. "Wow! I found my books!" Austin yelled (both then and during our interview), likely drawing the scolding disdain of several ancient librarians.

It was like a lightbulb went off in his brain and he could reconnect with himself. All of the work Austin believed to be swallowed or invented by his mental illness was there, perfectly placed in the university library. Austin had placed the final puzzle piece of his identity, reaffirming his selfhood that he so sorely missed.

But for Austin, the significance of this day extends beyond a single aspect of his life, even one as fundamental to him as writing. Just as Ernest had baselessly predicted six years ago, Austin realized the substantial positive impact that medication could have on his life.

The second after Austin found his books, he catapulted himself straight to the office of Dr. Rosenstock, clumsily stumbling from moving so fast and excitedly. Rosenstock then remarked that Austin's "eyes were more colourful than ever before" – to this day, a memory the physician holds in high regard. The medications helped Austin illuminate the grey, shadowy, and phantom realm of schizophrenic hallucinations with the dynamic colours of reality. That day, Austin knew that his decision to comply with medication was paramount to his functioning, and he has been on it consistently for almost 25 years.

As the tapestry of Austin's life continued to be stitched back together, he was finally ready to address another missing tear in the seams: education. Specifically, Austin wanted to pursue a doctorate degree. "I found the cheapest PhD program I could find on the back of the Economist. It was pretty ropey, but I thought, 'who knows how it'll go?'" Austin explains. "I got my thesis defence in 2000 on Alberta political networks in the legislature and Federal government over 100 years. But I had to rewrite my thesis over and over. I thought I was going to have a nervous breakdown – I couldn't have done that before Risperidone."

Certainly, Austin would face many trials and tribulations in the future – stigma, financial difficulty, and divorce, to name a few – but the fact was that he was buoyed by a strong foundation, and became more resilient as a person with schizophrenia than he ever had been before. The inches forward he made in the hospital continued to gain momentum and inertia, leading to Austin's new mantra: never give up, never surrender.

The man truly lives it – I cannot tell you how many times I've heard him declare the famous Independence Day quote, "we will not go quietly into the night" – usually when he gets a grand ambition to hire another 100 students or some other ridiculously lofty urge. He usually says the phrase somewhat jokingly, but to me, it speaks volumes about the kind of man he is. "I could have gone quietly and sunk into anonymity," says Austin. "Instead, I raged."

Raging against the dying light, Austin gathered all the treasures, accolades, and adornments from his journey into the underworld, and used them as sword and shield to battle the dragon of schizophrenia. He strove against the darkness and passed his trial by fire. Fighting fire with fire, he learned to recuperate his identity despite his schizophrenia and the chaos left in its wake and to reorder his world into something greater than it was before.

What Now?

"A Book of Verses underneath the Bough / A Jug of Wine, a Loaf of Bread – and Thou /
Beside me singing in the Wilderness / Oh, Wilderness were Paradise enow!"
Omar Khayyám, Rubáiyát of Omar Khayyám

After everything – the isolated childhood, the frozen wasteland, the kidnapping, the homelessness and abandonment, after everything – Austin believes he has had "such an unbelievable life." At one point, many people, including himself, thought his life was over; but it was the start of something new. He met his brilliant wife, adopted children, paid off his house, bought a dog, and started a completely new career. It was everything that everyone told him he would never have because of his schizophrenia. He considered the diagnosis a challenge of sorts – motivation to fuel his comeback and realize his new dream. "I think I have a unique perspective on life because of everything I went through," says Austin.

Austin found that one advantage of having endless downtime was being able to reassess his priorities. He lost so much throughout this transition, but at the same time gained more love than he ever imagined possible. "I feel very rich," says Austin. "I think that maybe we have lost that in society. People think they are rich when they have physical things, but really, I'm very rich – a millionaire in terms of social fabric and relationships. A lot of people don't have that."

Austin is no "Material Girl." You wouldn't see him driving around the city in a Lexus, brandishing designer clothes or slamming back an eight dollar frappuccino. Ultimately, Austin concluded that relationships were the only treasure he really needed. And while Austin jokes that relationships with girls seem to be his Achilles heel, he yearns for it all: Platonic, familial, professional – community. And he has accomplished this, establishing an empire of connections that mutually benefit from each other through

67

work, education, medicine, socialization, and, most importantly, love.

It all adds to one of the most extraordinary lives I have personally witnessed. Certainly, his worldly experiences don't disappoint, and he knows it. He laughs about his times in Antarctica, saying, "I unearthed a meteorite when urinating in Antarctica, I've never met anybody else in my whole life who's done that!"

Or when Austin and his fellow expedition members would play "tag" on snowmobiles to keep themselves entertained. In a fit of giggles, Austin recalls, "we would drive up to the other guy on his snowmobile and punch him in the shoulder driving 40km an hour across Antarctica!"

It's all to say that we can't think of anyone armed with as many eyebrow-raising anecdotes as Austin has, but the significance of that fact extends miles further than a laugh or two. "The reality of my life is more extraordinary than a lot of people's delusions," says Austin.

Given the context of this book, that's a big statement. Delusions are powerful transcendents of reality, often overtaking people like a soul-sucking dementor. Yet, Austin's reality is extraordinary in a different sense. Austin's reality is truer and more real than the ordinary life because it expresses the radical changes, decisions, and hardships that people contend with, which brings them face-to-face with the world in a way 'ordinary' life does not.

Now, there's a temptation to typecast Austin as some mystical guru full of wisdom and perseverance (he totally is), but his story demonstrates the immense value in cooperating with treatments and having an indomitable will to move in a direction. "Life doesn't have to be over. There are no guarantees, but you don't know the future," Austin preaches. "You just have to cooperate with the program and cooperate with the doctors – at least for some stuff. But even then, you can't just take meds for 50 years and expect to have a life. Doctors can't teach you to do that. If you want to have a life, you need to make it happen."

Austin wants people to know that the medication works. It can be very difficult to seek treatment because of fear and the underlying stigma in our society. But Austin witnessed his mother's chaotic life dealing with unmedicated schizophrenia and knew that avoiding the stigma just wasn't worth it. Going onto medication does not make you a weak person – in fact, you are strong enough to realize something needs to be done. It can be empowering to take control of your own life, your path, your destiny. Austin notes, "that's the choice I made. I made that choice and I obviously chose wisely."

And yet, medication alone will not pull your life back together. So, Austin took control of his destiny when he seemed doomed to fall silently into the abyss, and now he is an exemplar of success. He is a chairman for multiple non-profits, including the one we, as authors, were hired through – the Antarctic Institute of Canada (AIC). It is a program that Austin built from the ground up to help students build their portfolios and resumes with publications. As of July 2020, he has just under 35 students writing books and articles and is currently organizing through the Candian Student Service Grant (CSSG) to employ another 100 student volunteers in their fight against COVID-19. It is unbelievable what AIC has grown to be, and the mammoth it will become in the future.

The Antarctic Institute of Canada should not exist in the real world. It comes with an immense workload and is not a profitable enterprise (ironically, he loses money paying for the accounting to sign the students' cheques). Nonetheless, Austin and Catherine spend the entire year organizing this program for students to work for during their summers off. He understands the immense pressure of being a student and wants everyone to succeed in their field. Consequently, he is a professional mentor for many of the students and insists on using the status he had to fight for to issue every single student a recommendation to help us get a job or go into grad school. And it works.

Austin's list of awards is daunting and hard to count. Some of these achievements include the Caring Canadian Award in 1996 for his work with Unsung Heroes and for founding the Prosper Place Clubhouse, for which he was the first president for nearly 14 years. He won his first Golden Jubilee Award in 2002, and a second Diamond Jubilee Award in 2012 – both for his advocacy towards people who are mentally ill and disabled. Austin's most cherished award was the Order of Canada, which was given to him in 2006 for his willingness to talk openly of his own mental illness and the importance of medication. This national recognition brought a tremendous amount of awareness to mental health and mental health services to the country.

Now that the glamour of the Order of Canada and all the speeches has worn off, Austin has started to pursue other goals in life. One of his silliest goals (and my personal favourite) is to become "the most rejected guy in the world."

Ironically, Guinness World of Records rejected him for the request. In recalling the motivation behind this bizarre little episode, Austin laughs, saying, "Ernie Selenski, in the 90s, wrote The Joy of Not Working. He said that 'I was failing my way to success.'"

Clearly, that resonated with Austin. Although he has had hundreds of books published and endless amounts of articles, which is undoubtedly impressive, Austin has also had over 500 rejections for many of his other publications.

He laughs about how people think authors have this perfect lifestyle, making lots of money and releasing these profound works of art. But Austin just likes to write. "Everybody thinks that books should always be perfect, be spelt correctly, or look correct, but that's not how it works," Austin says.

He has set a goal to have over 1000 articles published and reach 200 published books, not including second editions and translations. If you include those, he's already surpassed it. He hopes that the AIC writing internship continues to grow, so he can continue to help students reach their full potential.

He is an author, scientist, a devout Catholic, husband, father, mentor, chairman of a non-profit, and most importantly, a great friend. Not bad for a guy who was destined to be the total sum of a dead man. The truth was just the opposite.

"I feel that maybe I was cursed and blessed," Austin says. "I mean, I was once cursed by schizophrenia, but 10 times blessed otherwise."

Austin's life echoed that of a phoenix. Just as he began to spread his wings, the curse of schizophrenia burnt him to a crisp. However, the blessing that came with his illness was his ability to rise again from his own ashes with a wider wingspan lifting him to higher altitudes, greater vantage points, and a new path forged in the flames of his past.

Epilogue: What Now? Again.

"Brey, you know what would be hilarious?
If we ended the book with the dog throwing up."
Zachary Schauer, Dark Night Cometh

It's inspiring to see such an eccentric, warm, and humble schizophrenic live this grandiose life that rivals epic poems in their imagery, and classic novels in their compelling messages of hope and growth. After his adventure through the lands of unreality and a period of intense personal growth, Austin's life and organizations continue to expand from the comfort of his home.

Whether you are a student working for his internship, or a plumber coming to fix the leak that flooded his apartment, it can be hard to see past the rough exterior of his life. The neighbourhood - ironically unneighbourly, the clutter, and the singing dog often mystify newcomers. Regardless, the Mardon's are quick to impress those lucky enough to enter their self-made community - to which the door is almost always open.

For students like us, writing books and articles for the Antarctic Institute of Canada, we are initiated into the organization by learning the ways of our very eccentric boss. Learning to interpret Austin's coded messages that arrive at any time of day or night is often most crucial. From having four missed calls at 8:00 am on a Saturday, to ambiguous texts saying "call John" (you don't know who John is), and certainly the mysterious – and easily misinterpreted – 2:00 am text saying "are you up?" - Austin's communication choices keep us on our toes.

Most days you'll find him scrambling to send emails or incessantly calling politicians, convincing them to donate money to nonprofits and charities (quite successfully, might I add). Austin's world seems trite and humorous on the outside, but in reality, it is incredibly fruitful and wondrous.

But alas, a book about Austin wouldn't capture the humorous tone underlying his life if it didn't give a snapshot of his day-to-day existence. During an interview for this book, Austin was forced to defer answering a question about his mother;

"The dog is ready to throw up," Austin urgently interjects before turning away from the webcam towards his dog, Ollie, who is just out of sight.

"Don't throw up on me," he pleads.

Riley, our interviewer, taken by surprise, grins and parses a little "uh-oh."

"Here, Ollie... Wanna grab the dog, Stanley? Oh drat! Grab a towel, he threw up!" Austin narrates, giving us his best mid-kerfuffle play-by-play.

Riley shuffles to hide his laughing under his breath, covering his face indiscreetly. He jests, "well, I'm glad this moment has been immortalized in the form of a video interview."

Austin giggles, "what is Brey going to think about the interview with the vomiting? Is she going to insert 'vomiting dog' in the transcript for the book?"

Riley, unaware of the power Brey has over this book, responded, "I think she may take the opportunity to skip a few minutes."

The joke is on you, Riley, here I am. Here is that scene, and here is the end of the book.

www.ingramcontent.com/pod-product-compliance
Lightning Source LLC
Chambersburg PA
CBHW030853270326
41928CB00008B/1358